IMAGES
of America

WHITE SANDS
NATIONAL
MONUMENT

IMAGES
of America

WHITE SANDS NATIONAL MONUMENT

Joseph T. Page II

ARCADIA
PUBLISHING

Published by Arcadia Publishing
Charleston, South Carolina

Printed in the United States of America

Library of Congress Control Number: 2013946957

For all general information, please contact Arcadia Publishing:
Telephone 843-853-2070
Fax 843-853-0044
E-mail sales@arcadiapublishing.com
For customer service and orders:
Toll-Free 1-888-313-2665

Visit us on the Internet at www.arcadiapublishing.com

To Melissa O'Brien Shroka (1978–2013).
Always a true friend, ready with a smile, hug, and a
sympathetic ear. Know that you are missed.

CONTENTS

ACKNOWLEDGMENTS

This project could not have been completed without the help of the National Park Service's White Sands National Monument (WSNM) team: Superintendent Marie Frias-Sauter, Chief of Natural and Cultural Resources David Bustos, Chief of Interpretation Rebecca Wiles, and Western National Parks Association's park store manager Anette Dunshee.

I'd also like to thank the following for their invaluable assistance: Jean Ann Killer and Don Larson (Tularosa Basin Historical Society); Director Chris Orwoll, George House, and Mike Shinaberry (New Mexico Museum of Space History); Director Darren Court (White Sands Missile Range Museum); and Erin E. Gaberlavage, for donation of her amazing photographs.

Thanks to Stacia Bannerman and all of the professionals at Arcadia Publishing for taking a chance on this book.

Thank you to my wife, Kim, for being my soul mate and nexus during this project; thank you to my children, for keeping me centered and distracted at the right times; thank you to my sister Erin and brother-in-law Robert, for sharing the New Mexican experience with me; and thank you to my parents, Joe and Kathy, for love and support.

Unless otherwise credited, all photographs are from White Sands National Monument's photographic archive. Any errors within the text are the sole responsibility of the author.

INTRODUCTION

Formal recognition of the uniqueness of the white sand gypsum dune field in southern New Mexico occurred on January 18, 1933, when Pres. Herbert Hoover, acting under the authority of the Antiquities Act of 1906, proclaimed and established a White Sands National Monument. The monument's story, however, can be traced to the waning years of the 19th century and is linked to the nationwide growth of the "national park" idea that followed the establishment of Yellowstone National Park in 1872.

The year 1876 marked the grand centennial for the United States, and the young nation was concerned about a perceived lack of a cultural heritage to equal the European standard. Unable to match the traditional measures of art, architecture, or literature, American nationalists seized upon the grand scenic vistas, particularly found in the American West, as a source of national pride. As the century neared its close, these treasures were increasingly included in national parks.

The economic benefit derived from park status was not lost on early promoters either. Parks brought visitors who would require a variety of services that translated into businesses and jobs. Following the Yellowstone Act, other park proposals proliferated as politicians sought a similar resource for their districts. Southern New Mexico is no exception. As early as 1898, a Sacramento Mountains National Park was suggested, but when organizers learned that their desire for a hunting preserve did not fit with the national park mission, the direction changed and the area became part of the Lincoln Forest Preserve in 1902.

The next national park notion surfaced in 1912 in the form of a bill sponsored by newly appointed senator A.B. Fall. His suggestion for a Mescalero National Park did not receive much support, but it kept the idea alive. By 1921, Senator Fall had moved on to the position of secretary of the interior and proposed the most ambitious park plan to date. The idea was to form an "all-weather national park" from a variety of public and private lands including a part of the Mescalero Indian Reservation, the Malpais lava flow near Carrizozo, all of the white sands dune field, White Mountain, and Elephant Butte Reservoir and lake. This idea managed to offend almost everybody and the plan quickly faded, but it did focus attention on the dune field, which was judged the one component with real potential for park status.

That potential coincided with the dream of a determined group of local promoters who had long sought to attract development in the Alamogordo area to capitalize on the dune resource. Many proposals had been submitted regarding commercial development of the gypsum found in the dunes.

The enthusiasm of Tom Charles, one of the leaders of the boosters, for the project was contagious and his perceptions about the value of the dunes were proved accurate. Interest in national recognition for the resource grew throughout the latter part of the 1920s. Studies were conducted by the National Park Service, which determined that while the dunes might not meet the criteria for national park status, which required a variety of resource values, the setting was ideal for preservation as a national monument. With the full backing of the New Mexico congressional delegation, as well as the support of communities from El Paso to Roswell, success was achieved in the waning hours of the Hoover administration.

In some ways the timing was fortuitous, for the establishment of the monument coincided with the dark days of the Great Depression and the economic recovery programs of the Roosevelt administration. Works Progress Administration (WPA) funds were used to improve many park areas, and White Sands benefited by achieving a full measure of development within just a few years of opening. Construction projects included the visitor center/administrative building, maintenance facilities, public restrooms, and park residences. All of these buildings are still in service.

As evidenced by visitation numbers over the decades, interest in the monument is proof of the clear vision shown by early park boosters. In its first year, the area attracted 12,000 people. By 1948, the number increased to more than 100,000 per year. The year 1957 marked the first time that visitation topped 300,000, and by 1965, more than 500,000 people were coming to the park each year. In four different years, total visitation has exceeded 600,000, the last time as recently as 1986.

Today and in the future, the park staff faces challenges meeting increased demand for services that ever-increasing visitation requires, including ensuring the protection of the resources for which the monument was established. In the months ahead, the park will be revising its management documents in an attempt to come to grips with this "preservation vs. use" dichotomy. Public input is an important part of this process, particularly on the role of the park in the local economy. The park will also examine its role as a living laboratory for desert research; the potential for new research in paleontology, archeology, and rapid adaptations in desert ecology; and new ways to provide for visitor interaction with desert resources. Further information on this process and the occasions for public involvement will be forthcoming. Local residents are urged to take advantage of these opportunities to help set future directions for this unique and very special place.

The visitor center building complex at White Sands National Monument is an excellent example of Spanish pueblo-adobe (Pueblo-Revival) architecture constructed during the years of the Depression. Construction began in 1936 and was completed in 1938 by various government agencies, including the WPA, at a cost of $31,600.

The walls of the visitor center are constructed entirely of adobe bricks. The bricks are usually 16 inches long, 10 inches wide, and 4 inches thick. Ordinarily, two men can mix and mold over 100 bricks in a day. There are various "recipes" for making adobe, and most include straw to prevent the bricks from cracking as they dry in the sun. Adobe buildings are not particularly durable unless regularly maintained. If the stucco facing covering the adobe bricks is damaged, the erosive forces of wind and rain quickly destroy the exposed mud bricks. Also, annual rainfall in excess of 20 inches (White Sands averages about eight inches) will endanger the adobe structure, since dampness tends to permeate and weaken the bases of the walls. Although research indicates that adobe is inferior to modern insulation materials, the interior of adobe structures seem cooler than other buildings.

The interior of the visitor center presents various examples of artistry in construction and furnishings. The ceiling in the main room is of *viga* and *savina* construction. The vigas are the large pine logs that form the main support for the roof. The decorative carved scrolls on which the vigas rest are called corbels, which serve to distribute the weight of the roof to the walls. Running at right angles on top of the vigas are groups of three aspen poles called savinas. On top of the savinas is a split wood covering. Completely authentic roofs are made of brush and several feet of compacted dirt—the visitor center roof is modern tar and gravel.

Benches and chairs are typical Indian-Spanish design, being heavily constructed to resist splitting and loosening due to humidity or dryness. Decorative carving on the furniture is modest but typical for the period.

The light fixtures are made of tinware. Tin was a poor man's substitute for silver on the Spanish-Mexican frontier. Each village had at least one tinsmith, and often individuals crafted their own tinware since all that was needed was a nail to punch holes and something to cut the sheet of tin. Designs on tinware in New Mexico show a strong New England influence, probably due to trade with the United States over the Santa Fe Trail.

One of the most prized articles of trade to reach frontier New Mexico was glass, which was so valuable that it was seldom used for windows. It was used instead for covering pictures of saints or was decorated with painted designs and framed with tin. One of the most common methods of decorating glass was to paint one side and draw a common hair comb over the painted surface before it dried, thus creating "combed glass." Examples of combed glass can be seen in the light fixtures near the front entrance.

The White Sands National Monument Historic District, including the visitor center and adjacent seven buildings built between 1936 and 1940, was officially listed in the National Register of Historic Places in 1988.

Set in a landscape of native plants, the historic district preserves this unique architectural style and is a tribute to the plans of the architects and the fine craftsmanship of the WPA workers.

Lyle Bennett, the principal architect for the White Sands Visitor Center, began architectural work for the National Park Service in the 1930s. He became a master of the Pueblo-Revival style, as demonstrated at White Sands. He also designed the Painted Desert Inn at Petrified Forest National Park, the historic district at Bandelier National Monument, and buildings at Carlsbad Caverns and Mesa Verde National Parks. Designer Robert W. Alders was also heavily involved in the design of the buildings.

One

HEART OF THE
TULAROSA BASIN

Viewable from space and sandwiched between the San Andres and Sacramento Mountain ranges, the patch of white gypsum dunes truly exists as the heart of the Tularosa Basin. Inspiration for artists, businessmen, warriors, explorers, and scientists alike, the area has provided hope and promise for many of these same groups throughout its history. Some of these dreams have panned out; others have faded into the wind.

Early New Mexican historical figures such as Gov. Miguel Antonio Otero pushed the interests of the area's resource potential through rigorous education and scientific study. Volumes of scientific papers on the white sands gypsum flowed from the state's renowned higher education institutions (New Mexico State University, New Mexico Institute of Mining Technology, and University of New Mexico) during the last years of the 19th century through the first two decades of the 20th century. Increased attention on the area allowed local personalities like Tom Charles to petition for the creation of a national park in the region. Economic interest was pushed in the form of a chemical processing plant, with plans to derive agricultural fertilizer, plaster of Paris, and sulphuric acid from the plentiful gypsum reserves. Plans to fully tap the chemical resources were less than successful, mostly due to low market demand for gypsum and high transportation costs. However, the political interest in a regional attraction spurred by the possible economic boon persisted through the 1920s and 1930s.

The resulting monument anchored the tourism draw to the Alamogordo area and surrounding mountain villages of Cloudcroft and Ruidoso. The Tularosa Basin's figurative "heart" continues to command the attention of the aforementioned artists, warriors, and scientists, as well as the average citizen. In the decades since its inception, thousands of visitors stream along New Mexico's Highway 70 to see the other-worldly views within the monument's boundaries.

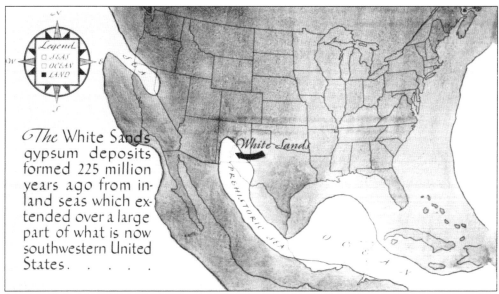

The White Sands gypsum deposits formed 225 million years ago from inland seas which extended over a large part of what is now southwestern United States. . . . .

This map shows the North American landmass during the formation of the area that would become White Sands National Monument 225 million years ago, overlaid with the continent's present-day outline.

Two children romp down a sand dune at WSNM while a soaptree yucca (*Yucca elata*) survives against the overwhelming odds buried beneath the gypsum. The photograph highlights the juxtaposition of the monument's character as both a place of carefree recreation and a location of scientific study into Mother Nature's survival instincts.

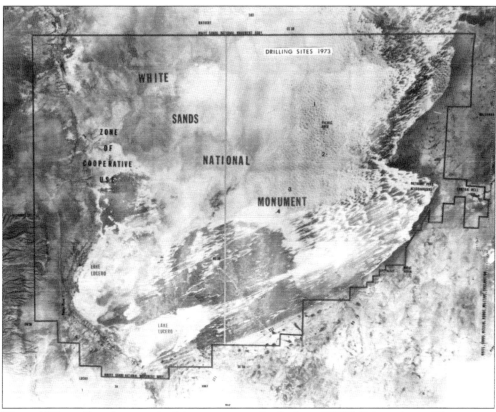

This c. 1973 satellite photograph of the monument clearly shows WSNM's boundaries. The western area, delineated by a wholly appropriate thin gray line, is labeled "Zone of Cooperative Use."

Park ranger Robert Morris looks for lost hikers across the northwest portion of the monument while the San Andres range provides a backdrop on January 17, 1959. The idyllic landscape is very deceptive to hikers. In 1849, Army captain Randolph B. Marcy noted that the Sacramento Mountains "[did not] appear to be greater distance than eight to ten miles." In actuality, they were more than 40 miles from his location.

A group of Army wives lies in a starburst pose at WSNM. During the years of World War II, visits by the United Services Organization (USO) for morale purposes were common. Soldiers and their significant others would travel from Fort Bliss, Texas, about 100 miles south, or Alamogordo Army Airfield, just six miles east, to visit the eye-catching sands

Beautifully portrayed in this photograph, the purity of the sands is evident. A hydrous form of calcium sulfate, gypsum is rarely found in the form of sand because it is water soluble. Normally, dissolved gypsum would follow flowing water routes to the sea. Since water does not exit the Tularosa Basin, like a bathtub with no drain, the dissolved gypsum and other sediments are trapped there.

14

An Army Corps of Engineers bulldozer slices through a dune in preparation for geologic study. While ostensibly for peaceful scientific purposes, the Army's desire to participate in trenching activities filled gaps in its topographic knowledge. Conflicts such as the Yom Kippur War in 1973 showed how constructed sand berms would slow down an advancing enemy, in addition to how sand obstacles could be overcome by a clever force. (Courtesy of US Geological Survey Photographic Library.)

Geologists on ladders investigate the strata of a barchans dune in 1963. Studies initiated during the International Geophysical Year (1957–1958) brought advances to the study of 11 unique earth sciences. The reinvigorated study of geologic processes into the next decade brought scientists to WSNM to cut through a gypsum dune and study the layers within. (Courtesy of US Geological Survey Photographic Library.)

A scientist studies strata at the bottom of a trenched sand dune at White Sands around 1963. The resident geologist at WSNM, Dr. Edwin McKee, believed that the dunes were covered over by subsequent layers of each successively created dune. During his research, he drilled into the dunes and discovered they averaged only 30 feet thick. (Courtesy of US Geological Survey Photographic Library.)

This photograph, taken by the Army Air Service in 1925, shows hundreds of transverse dune crests in the gypsum fields. The Army Air Service was the forerunner to the Army Air Forces and, later, the US Air Force. While this may have been the earliest, if not the first photograph of a military aircraft over the sands, it is certainly not the last. (Courtesy of US Geological Survey Photographic Library.)

Hikers make their way across the dunes, as photographed from an Air Force aircraft in the 1960s. The relationship between the National Park Service and the Department of Defense entities inside the Tularosa Basin is explored in a later chapter; however, when the lives of wayward hikers are at stake, rescue efforts are fully cooperative and coordinated, much to the benefit of the rescued.

The White Sands Balloon Invitational is an annual event that precedes the October International Balloon Fiesta in Albuquerque. Many balloon crews partake in order to experience the unusual environment, distinguished not only by the color and texture of the surroundings, but also the airspace above. White Sands Missile Range controls the air traffic above the Tularosa Basin, so opportunities for civilian air crews to fly over the great white sands are limited to medical evacuation flights and special events such as this.

This c. 1965 automobile accident shows travel up a dune. Aside from obvious damage to automobiles off-roading at high speed, the sands' rigidity varies between soft and hard pack. The difference is not always obvious to the casual observer, so unwise off-road adventurers may find themselves the next fool stuck in the sand.

Boy Scouts from Troop No. 144 clamor to gather trash bags out of a pickup truck. The monument has been a popular stop for Scouting adventures ranging from day hikes to overnight stays. The fortuitous timing of one lucky local troop earned them the Adopt-a-Highway cleanup spot directly adjacent to the monument on Highway 70.

This car commercial, featuring the Clenet Coachworks Series II Cabriolet, was filmed at the monument in 1986. The company produced limited-edition luxury automobiles from its plant in Santa Barbara, California. The average price of the Series II hovered around $100,000 by the end of its production run. According to NPS documents, it is estimated that 90 percent of all automobile makes and models have been to WSNM for commercial filming or photography.

A touring car from the White Sands Service Company crests a dune. The touring company was the brainchild of then-retired monument superintendent Tom Charles. In 1939, Charles attempted to negotiate his post-retirement plans with NPS to include operating a concession and touring business with no competition from other vendors. As a compromise, NPS agreed to a mobile food/souvenir trailer, which Charles could tow into the dunes each morning.

Ashley and Chris Gardini's "Jumping around the World" photographic series began one afternoon in Barcelona's Parc Güell as a humorous way to record their travels. Since its conception, the photo series has documented locations on three continents, including the spectacular White Sands National Monument in 2011. (Courtesy of Ashley and Chris Gardini.)

Three models in swimwear pose at WSNM. Weather within the Tularosa Basin is deceptive at certain times of the year. The white gypsum reflects heat extremely well, giving the monument a noticeable temperature difference from its surroundings. It is not unheard of to experience 60-degree temperatures in the Sacramento Mountains, almost 90 degrees inside the city limits of Alamogordo, and mid-70s inside the monument, all within the same day!

This behind-the-scenes shot shows photographers with models in swimsuits. WSNM has been a popular destination to film, with 23 movies and 9 music videos filmed on-location. The monument has represented an alien planet (*The Man Who Fell to Earth*, 1976), the deserts of Qatar (*Transformers*, 2007), and an Old West town (*Hang Em High*, 1968), among others.

A small tribe of children and their loyal dog scurry up a dune. The idea that a simple pile of white sand can occupy visitors of all ages is mind-boggling until one steps on the crest of a dune and gazes at the beauty around them. The monument draws a steady stream of visitors, frequently topping over 450,000 annually.

A fearless young woman attempts to ski down a slope. Sled-riding is just one of the activities attempted by guests. Visiting groups have been known to have contests for the best sled design. Aesthetics and physics aside, the best sleds are usually the simplest—a piece of cardboard or plastic disk (available at the visitor center gift shop).

Scrawled "graffiti" indicates the author was from, or had some connection to, the state of Iowa. Unlike the sand along an ocean or lake, which has a high percentage of moisture and can retain its integrity for the construction of simple structures, the monument's gypsum is difficult to build into any discernible formation. Consequently, writing in the sands is very popular. For legibility from a distance, the letters are often 10 feet high.

Die-Cut Sticker

WHITE SANDS
National Park

Rising in a seemingly endless procession from an ancient lake bed in the Tularosa Basin of southern New Mexico, the stark gypsum dunes of White Sands National Park grow, crest, and slump, driven by the wind. The sands form an ecological island where desert plants and animals have adapted to a bright and shifting world.

7 44252 21434 0

Image #106650

Children wait in line to sip from a water truck on Play Day, April 13, 1946. Water is a rare commodity in the desert. While restroom facilities are present along Dunes Drive, potable water must be carried in by visitors, campers, and hikers.

A group of young women make their final strokes during an improvised round of golf. While there are a few 9- and 18-hole courses within 50 miles, no official course exists at the monument. The folly of playing the sport in the white sands becomes evident when considering the color of most golf balls. Thankfully, these ladies came prepared with dark colored balls.

A woman tees off during an impromptu golf game inside the monument. In 1987, New Mexico State University, in nearby Las Cruces, was the third educational institution in the United States to offer a professional golf management degree. Popularity of the game inside the monument, however, has waned considerably, most likely due to the course's sizable sand traps.

Two young children slide down the dunes. (Courtesy of Page family, New Mexico chapter.)

The moon rises over the desertscape. One of the programs offered by WSNM is the full-moon hike. The viewing environment is similar to twilight in dawn or evening hours, complete with shadows. The illumination upon the sands provides visitors a once-in-a-lifetime experience, aptly summed up in the seasonal poem *The Night Before Christmas*: "The moon on the breast of the new-fallen snow / Gave the lustre of mid-day to objects below." (Courtesy of Erin E. Gaberlavage.)

Two

CREATION OF
A MONUMENT

In 1898, a group of El Paso investors wanted to establish a 12-square-mile "Mescalero National Park" inside the edge of the Mescalero Indian Reservation, northeast of the sands. On three separate occasions, the US Congress rejected Sen. Albert Fall's proposals to create a park in southern New Mexico, owing mostly to Fall's corrupt means used to gain the land from native tribes. When the National Park Service decided to create the monument in 1933, it was an amalgamation of many different views of what kind of national park should be created in southwest New Mexico.

The monument has had very experienced individuals serve as custodians and later superintendents. These individuals include Thomas "Tom" Charles (1933–1939), Johnwill Faris (1939–1961), Forrest M. Benson Jr. (1961–1964), Donald A. Dayton (1964–1967), John F. Turney (1967–1973), James M. Thompson (1973–1978), Donald R. Harper (1978–1988), Dennis Ditmanson (1989–1997), Dennis A. Vasquez (1997–2000), Jim Mack (2000–2003), Cliff Spencer (2003–2007), Kevin Schneider (2007–2012), and Marie Frias Sauter (2012–present).

Many interesting anecdotes are captured in Dr. Dietmar Schiender-Hector's seminal text, "White Sands: History of a National Monument," and Michael Welsh's "Dunes and Dreams: A History of White Sands National Monument." The steadfastness of purpose in maintaining the monument's sovereignty against military and political forces is wholly displayed many times over in the written words of these courageous individuals, as documented by Schneider-Hector and Welsh.

Welcoming visitors to the dunes is the iconic White Sands National Monument sign. Though the sign has changed throughout the years, its intent has stayed the same.

The Civilian Conservation Corps (CCC) built many of the facilities at White Sands National Monument. The CCC was established as a public relief work program in 1933.

Taken April 29, 1934, this picture shows the large crowd of visitors who came out to celebrate Founder's Day at White Sands National Monument. The event paid homage to the local community members and families who had a hand in the creation of the park and success of nearby Alamogordo.

Often referred to as the Father of White Sands, Tom Charles fine-tuned Albert Falls's vision of a yearlong playground. Pictured here is Tom Charles and his wife, Bula. The Fallses were lifelong supporters of the monument.

The small town of Alamogordo bred close friendships, and the individuals in this picture were the last of an era. Pictured in 1934 are Tom Charles (left) and L.L. Garton, owner of a local ranch.

In 1939, the museum ordered the creation of several dioramas to educate the public on the unique geology of the White Sands. Though no longer on display at the monument, the dioramas were a testament to the active role NPS staff takes in educating visitors.

The construction of the dioramas was an intensive process. The original diorama was in three separate large pieces. Only one is still intact today; it is currently in storage with the Tularosa Basin Historical Society in Alamogordo, New Mexico.

The inside of the current visitor center still retains its original structures. The corbels being constructed in this photograph are still very much visible today.

Lake Lucero is a major source of gypsum for White Sands National Monument. The gypsum that makes up the dunes comes from Lake Otero, which is the current Lake Lucero and Alkali Flats. Seen here are several individuals conducting studies on the qualities of the selenite crystals that are left after the waters evaporate. Selenite is the crystalline form of gypsum.

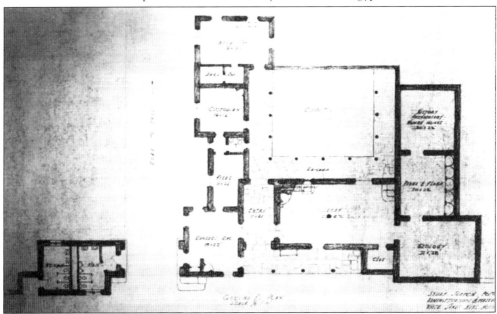

The original floor plan of the White Sands National Monument visitor center has changed little since its original construction. The basic layout seen here has changed only to accommodate offices. The dimensions of the building have not changed.

Individuals who worked at the White Sands National Monument did not necessarily have homes in the town of Alamogordo, located 15 miles away, and most did not own vehicles.

The structures of the White Sands National Monument are constructed to enhance rather than detract from the desert environment. To that extent, the buildings were constructed with adobe. Adobe is still used today in the Southwest; it withstands the natural desert environment nicely and blends seamlessly with the landscape.

This was the first "paved" road in the monument, built by the CCC. It was an experimental road made of clay. Vehicles are always cautioned to stay on marked roads and to be aware of standing water. Prior to areas of the monument being restricted for car use, individuals could take their chances exploring, with varying consequences.

For several years White Sands opened it gates for an annual Play Day. Members of the community would participate in monument-sponsored baseball games and cookouts, and even the local high school band would play.

Members from surrounding communities often travel just to visit the monument. Taken in June 1943, this photograph shows a USO-sponsored trip to White Sands National Monument for the Army wives of Fort Bliss in El Paso, Texas.

L.L. Garton was a local businessman in the Tularosa Basin. Garton's home was built beside a lake he created by drilling an artesian well in search of oil on his property.

Pictured in March 1948, the annual Field Day for local school children was a huge event for the youth. The festivities were sponsored by the Alamogordo Chamber of Commerce and included events for all ages.

The second "caretaker," Johnwill Faris, was first designated superintendent of the park. Faris struggled with the creation of a new monument. One of Faris's early, and constant, struggles was with the US military. Faris worked diligently to ensure that the park would remain open to visitors while still accommodating the military.

The crystalline shards that litter the bed of Lake Lucero are called selenite. Selenite is the crystal form of gypsum and is often transparent and clear but can also exist in amber, yellow, brown, and orange variations.

Taken from above, this photograph shows the layout of the entrance to White Sands National Monument, off Highway 70. The highway was realigned closer to the dunes sometime after this photograph was taken.

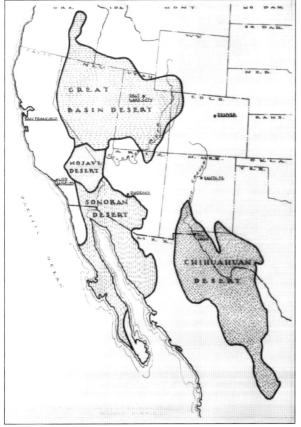

Pictured here is a map of the deserts of the Southwest. White Sands National Monument is in the Chihuahuan Desert, which is approximately 140,000 square miles and is speculated to be the most biologically diverse desert in the world.

The remains of this *carreta*, or cart, were found in 1973. Though modern people did not live within the dune area, they often traveled along its outskirts.

Pictured here is a reconstructed carreta. In 1973, the pieces of one were found near one of the roads in the park. The dunes are quick to shift, covering what was lost until the winds blow again and reveal their secrets.

The visitor center's entry has changed little since its construction in the 1930s. The upstairs has been walled off and is now a library of desert resources. The full windows in the back are now blocked by a wall and provide an entrance to a portion of the administration section.

Pictured here is the construction of the concessionaire portion of the visitor center. The first concessionaires were Tom and Bula Charles.

Contrary to popular belief, deserts do get snow. Typical lows in the winter months are in the mid- to high 20s, with a record low of 25 degrees below zero. Though heavy snowfall is uncommon, typically every year the monument gets at least a dusting of white snow on white sand.

The entranceway to the monument has changed over the years. The original pay stations have expanded to accommodate the individuals working the stations.

Tourists push a car out of a sand drift. The first road into the monument was completed in 1934, but not all areas were accessible by pavement. Adventure-seekers would attempt to bash through sand drifts, often with unpleasant outcomes.

Taken in December 1964, this photograph commemorates the 400,000th visitor to the monument. The photograph includes Mr. and Mrs. Charles Levsey, Mr. and Mrs. Allen Dossett, park superintendent Forest M. Benson, and Bruce Peterson.

A day at White Sands is a pleasant way to relax, have fun, and enjoy the sun. This family is prepared to stay the day. Shade has been provided, food is served, and the playpen is out to keep baby from wandering.

In December 1968, White Sands commemorated its 600,000th visitor. From left to right are a local newspaper photographer, park superintendent Turney, Bill Dunn, Mr. and Mrs. Edward R. Boyer, T.L. Womack, and Wes Walker.

Seasonal park rangers have always played a vital role in the functioning of the monument. Taken in 1974, this photograph of Kathy Hughes reflects the current fashion for female park rangers. Today, most park rangers wear pants to better accommodate their surroundings.

In January 1972, Secretary of the Interior Rogers Morton visited White Sands National Monument. Tribal members from the nearby Mescalero Apache Reservation greeted him.

This sign is for the c. 1965 campfire program. Later programs at the monument would include full-moon hikes and sunset strolls.

This is the inside of the visitor center in the 1970s. While the building's exterior remains the same, this room now contains the bookstore and visitor information desk. Displays and dioramas still line the walls, however.

Chief ranger Hugh Bozarth presents Supt. John F. Turney a going-away memento from White Sands Missile Range on November 11, 1973. Ranger Bozarth participated in many cooperative missile retrievals, as documented in chapter three. Turney's next NPS posting would be Padre Island National Seashore, Texas.

Fulfilling a childhood dream, hikers Loren Froemke (right) and Steve Studebaker (left) attempt to hike along the crest of the Rocky Mountains. Departing from the Canadian border on June 18, 1976, the pair arrived at WSNM and was photographed by chief ranger Robert Schumerth on November 25, 1976.

A park ranger rides atop his trusty steed, a popular method of transportation in the back country. Today, all-terrain vehicles have replaced horses for NPS employees; however, visitors can still bring pack animals under specific park regulations.

Supt. John Turney (October 6, 1967–December 8, 1973) presents an award to Bill Cunningham.

Here is a photograph of Supt. James M. Thomson (December 9, 1973–August 12, 1978). Thomson's tenure would see reinvigoration of the Trinity National Historic Site proposal and subsequent dismissal by the US Department of Defense. His actions earned high praise from Carl Walker, acting director of the NPS Southwest Region: "[Thomson] patiently and constructively healed the wounds and brought WSMR officials into the project as real participants."

A couple from El Paso, Texas, exchange marriage vows at WSNM, surrounded by family and friends in August 1975.

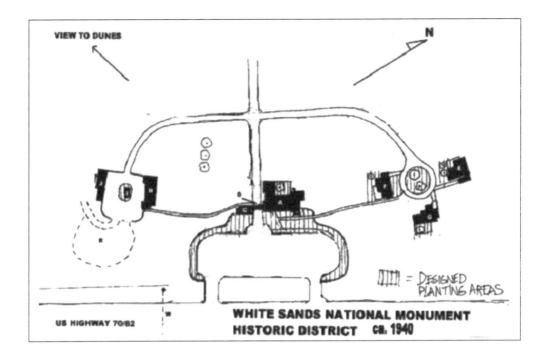

Here are two diagrams, one from the 1940s and the other from 1999, of the WSNM Historic District. Its expansion included an additional parking lot on the northern side and the creation of a third wall enclosing a courtyard next to the visitor center's main building.

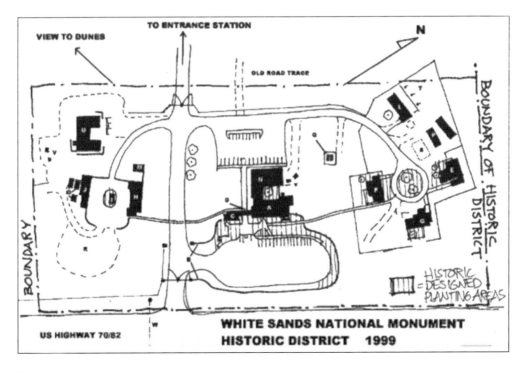

Park ranger Mary Jane Tate (center) stands with three generations of WSNM superintendents, from left to right, Don Dayton, Don Harper, and John Turney. Tate had worked with all three at different assignments throughout her career in the National Park Service, as well as being an acting superintendent at WSNM in 1989.

This view is from underneath the awning outside the visitor center. Outside the frame to the right is the White Sands Trading Company, a concessionaire that sells jewelry, fine gifts, food, and most importantly, plastic disks to slide down the sands.

University of Texas at El Paso student Marsha McKinnerney sets up a bait station inside the interdune flats in June 1976.

The inside of the visitor center shows the bookstore and visitor desk. In conjunction with the monument, the Western National Parks Association runs the bookstore. It holds an impressive collection of books about the monument and wildlife of the Chihuahuan Desert.

Above, chief of interpretation Rebecca Wiles poses in the early morning at the White Sands Balloon Invitational. At right, a balloon takes off from the monument.

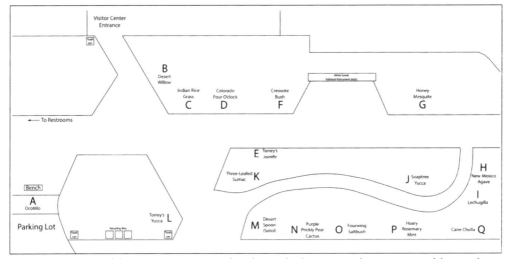

This line drawing of the visitor center's garden shows the locations of many types of desert plants displayed in their native habitat.

A scene from the movie *Year One* was filmed inside WSNM. Over 20 movies have been filmed at WSNM, with eight filmed from 2005 to 2008.

Here is a present-day view of the visitor center from the parking lot. While undergoing expansion and repairs since its initial construction, the structure's Southwestern charm has not been lost, maintaining a dark adobe finish and simple architectural design. (Courtesy of Page family, New Mexico chapter.)

The visitor center courtyard was originally designed with walls along two sides, giving the impression of a patio or backyard. Over time other buildings were added, such as the concessions at the White Sands Trading Post. (Courtesy of Melissa Wilde.)

Musicians Felipe Ruibal (left) and Luis Guerra of the band Quemozo stroll to their gig. The draw of the monument has brought musicians of all types to play their instruments in the sand. Well-known artists such as Boyz II Men, Pink Floyd, Sara Evans, and Martina McBride have filmed music videos at WSNM. (Courtesy of the National Park Service.)

Here is the White Sands National Monument boundary along Highway 70. The more obvious signs of white sand dunes are seen miles before, heading eastbound toward Alamogordo. (Courtesy of Page family, New Mexico chapter.)

During the month of December, luminaries are lit for an event at the visitor center. Known as "festival lights," modern luminaries are made from brown paper bags weighted with sand displaying a lit candle. (Courtesy of the National Park Service.)

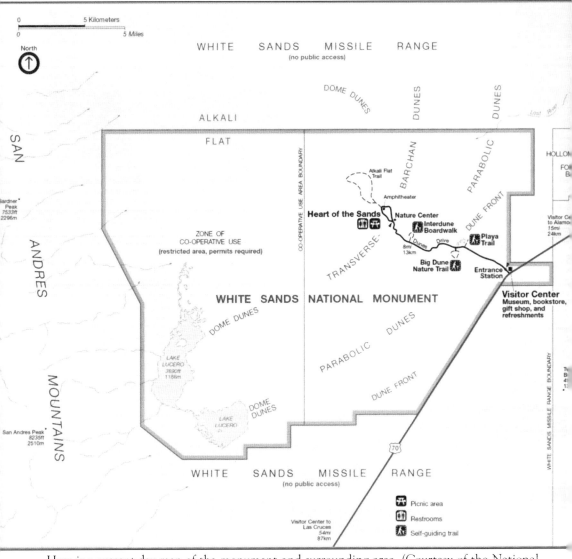

WHITE   SANDS   MISSILE   RANGE
(no public access)

DOME DUNES   DUNES   DUNES   Lost River

ALKALI

FLAT

SAN

Gardner
Peak
7533ft
2296m

ANDRES

MOUNTAINS

San Andres Peak
8235ft
2510m

Alkali Flat
Trail

Amphitheater

BARCHAN

PARABOLIC

DUNE FRONT

HOLLOM

FOR
B

Visitor Ce
to Alamo
15mi
24km

Heart of the Sands   Nature Center

TRANSVERSE

Interdune
Boardwalk

Dunes   Drive

Playa
Trail

8mi
13km

ZONE OF
CO-OPERATIVE USE
(restricted area, permits required)

Big Dune
Nature Trail

Entrance
Station

Visitor Center
Museum, bookstore,
gift shop, and
refreshments

CO-OPERATIVE USE AREA BOUNDARY

WHITE   SANDS   NATIONAL   MONUMENT

DOME DUNES

PARABOLIC   DUNES

LAKE
LUCERO
3890ft
1186m

DUNE FRONT

DOME
DUNES

LAKE
LUCERO

WHITE SANDS MISSILE RANGE BOUNDARY

Tu
B
4
1

70

WHITE   SANDS   MISSILE   RANGE
(no public access)

Visitor Center to
Las Cruces
54mi
87km

Picnic area

Restrooms

Self-guiding trail

0   5 Kilometers
0   5 Miles

North

Here is a present-day map of the monument and surrounding area. (Courtesy of the National
Park Service.)

62

Three

NEIGHBORS IN THE "WORLD'S LARGEST SHOOTING GALLERY"

Army records state that Lt. William F. Smith performed the first military reconnaissance of the white sands area in September 1849. His conclusions were a great disappointment to later adventurers and researchers due to a general lack of interest in the area. Decades would pass before the Army would tread these grounds again. Cavalry skirmishes with Apache in New Mexico during the 1880s Indian Wars would mark the only recorded military engagements within the Tularosa Basin.

Renewed interest in the early 20th century would find the military aimed at acquiring lands for training bomber crews and later testing weapon systems. In the name of national security, the US government co-opted thousands of acres of land from farmers and ranchers inside the Tularosa Basin. The lands were used to create Alamogordo Army Airfield (later, Holloman Air Force Base) and White Sands Proving Grounds (later, White Sands Missile Range). The descendants of the farmers and ranchers fought for decades to reclaim their family lands, to no avail. As military work in the basin increased during World War II and the Cold War, so did the threat of disturbing monument lands.

Writings from NPS personnel such as Johnwill Faris would wholly recognize the inequities of the situation: the monument's sovereignty stacked against the needs and desires of national security programs within the basin. As the decades wore on, the best of a bad situation in the "World's Largest Shooting Gallery" improved greatly. Progressive military members such as Major General J.F. Thorlin forced accountability on his subordinates for disturbing the sanctity of the monument; later commanders at Holloman and WSMR would follow suit.

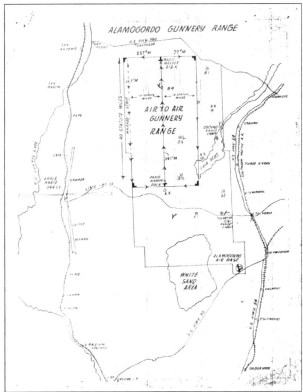

This map shows the outline of the Alamogordo Gunnery and Bombing Range in the early 1940s. Even after establishment in 1933 and almost a decade before the founding of Alamogordo Army Airfield, WSNM is relegated in Army documentation as "White Sand Area" and bisected by the range's perimeter. (Courtesy of 49th Wing History Office.)

B-24 Liberators fly westward over the Tularosa Basin. By far, the B-24 was the most common aircraft located at Alamogordo Army Airfield, with 10 bombardment groups calling the basin home during the early part of the 1940s. The wide open spaces of the New Mexico desert allowed crews to hone their finely crafted skills. (Courtesy of 49th Wing History Office.)

A B-24 Liberator flies over the visitor center in 1942. From 1942 to 1945, 14 bombardment groups flew the B-24 from the neighboring Alamogordo Army Airfield (AAF). Air crews were trained in many subjects, such as takeoffs and landings, navigation, and bombing accuracy. Sadly, over the same time period, there were 77 accidents with 171 fatalities on all aircraft at AAF, not just the B-24.

A B-24 Liberator flies over White Sands National Monument. Images of Army Air Forces aircraft flying inside the United States (or ZI, Zone of Interior) are rare due to the intense security restrictions placed upon personnel during World War II. Fortunately, enough AAF personnel violated these rules to provide wonderful images from this era. (Courtesy of 49th Wing History Office.)

This photograph from the Zone of Cooperative Use shows military debris around April 1964. The wreckage is of a World War II–era B-17 Flying Fortress converted into a remote-control target drone for use at Holloman Air Force Base. The 3225th Drone Squadron supported missile tests at White Sands Missile Range for numerous air-to-air missiles. In many cases, such as this, the missiles won the aerial battle.

A XQ-2 Firebee drone is dropped from a B-26 Invader over the gypsum fields. The 1st Tow Target Squadron from nearby Biggs Air Force Base routinely came to the Tularosa Basin to practice. (Courtesy of 49th Wing History Office.)

Exhausted infantry soldiers rest at the visitor center around 1942. A scale model of a carreta can be seen near the center of the photograph.

Infantry soldiers make the long march up a dune. It is unknown if these marches were prerequisite experience for future desert combat operations.

Army soldiers bivouac within the gypsum fields around 1942. (Courtesy of the Tularosa Basin Historical Society.)

The second launch and first fully successful flight of a V-2 rocket in the United States occurred at White Sands Proving Grounds on May 10, 1946. The rocket climbed straight up then pitched to the north, reaching an altitude of 71 miles and impacting 35 miles up range. (Courtesy of the WSMR Museum.)

V-2 rocket No. 59 lifts off from White Sands Proving Grounds. The impact of one particular V-2 brought an unintentionally humorous response from Superintendent Faris. When the Army was questioned about the unintentional impact in the monument, they denied it, stating the launch and impact on target was successful. Faris quipped that the Army was right, if the target was WSNM! Two months later the Army admitted the gaffe. (Courtesy of the WSMR Museum.)

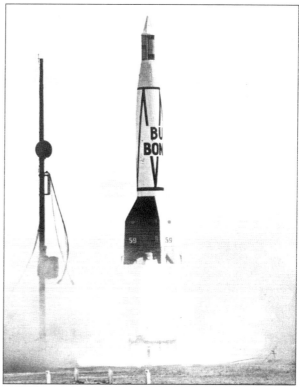

Children climb atop a V-2 rocket during an open house at the monument. Blatant military exhibitionism at WSNM would lessen considerably during the subsequent decades, following changes in relations between the NPS and Department of Defense.

This Vietnam-era M-113 Armored Personnel Carrier sits atop a gypsum mesa while the crew scouts its target. Tactics developed by mechanized vehicle crews in the 1970s and 1980s were put to the test during Operation Desert Storm in 1991. That engagement's overwhelming success can be directly attributed to desert exercises undertaken by Fort Bliss troops, such as the 3rd Armored Cavalry Regiment.

Renewed emphasis on desert warfare came to the forefront during the latter part of the 1960s. The Cold War antagonists' "battles of tomorrow" were fought by proxy in the Six-Day War (1967) and the Yom Kippur War (1973) with US and Soviet hardware going head-to-head.

Visiting soldiers from the Republic of Korea get water during a visit to the monument. Fort Bliss's main raison d'être has changed multiple times in the last 165 years. From Old West cavalry outpost to infantry and air defense training center, the base has been host to at least 28 Allied nations.

Visiting Allied troops stationed at Fort Bliss take a break from warfare studies to enjoy a little recreation. Since only a handful of gypsum dune fields exist around the world and White Sands' dune field is by far the world's largest, covering 275 square miles, it is a sure stop for any visitor.

The photograph to the left shows a Little Joe II rocket launched from WSMR's Launch Complex 36 during engineering tests. Engineering launches such as this allowed testing of the Apollo Launch Escape System (LES) prior to the moon missions of the late 1960s. LES motors would fire and pull the Apollo command module (CM) and astronauts away from a failed rocket during launch. Below, a boilerplate CM sits in the gypsum fields east of the monument. (Both, courtesy of NASA.)

A UH-1 Iroquois "Huey" military transport helicopter stands ready at the helipad near the visitor center. Once a frequent sight over the monument, UH-1s were used heavily during the Vietnam War era. One unique Huey, still in use at WSMR, is colloquially called a "flare copter" and shoots out hundreds of high intensity flares during flight.

A softball-sized projectile sits on the desert floor awaiting explosive ordnance disposal. Some munitions contain "bomblets," small sub-projectiles that shoot out over a wide area. It is unknown how many of these litter the basin, but estimates are in the tens of thousands.

A soldier repairs a small crater formed by falling debris on Highway 70. The highway bisects the Tularosa Basin and is the only direct line of transportation from White Sands Missile Range to Alamogordo.

In December 1975, a National Park Service representative (right) looks over an impact site near Lake Lucero.

Four UH-1 helicopters from Fort Bliss are seen landing near the visitor center on December 17, 1974. Helicopter flights are occasionally used for Army officer orientation around the Tularosa Basin. Records show the monument had only one documented battle during the 1880s Indian Wars; however, the basin was rife with small unit tactical maneuvers during that same decade. Students from Fort Bliss study the encounters in a classroom and then take a hands-on field trip.

Pictured are the results of a stray missile impact near WSNM. The first rocket launch took place at WSMR on September 25, 1945. Over 32,000 launches would take place throughout the next 35 years. The NPS's special use permit for the military requires unintentional impact areas within the monument be restored to their unblemished natural conditions.

Chief ranger Hugh H. Bozarth briefs two Army officers before entering WSNM. Special use permits were granted to the Army from the 1940s to the late 1970s. (Courtesy of the WSMR Museum.)

An OH-13 Sioux helicopter lifts debris from a Navy Talos missile under direction of chief ranger Hugh Bozarth. Upon notification of unauthorized military recovery into the monument, WSMR commander Major General J.F. Thorlin (1962–1965) imposed disciplinary action against the offending personnel. To negate further unauthorized entries, Army recovery crews would be escorted by a WSNM ranger. (Both, courtesy of the WSMR Museum.)

Military personnel and civilian engineers work to disarm a missile airframe prior to the start of recovery. Even after a bone-jarring launch and earth shattering impact, rocket and missile airframes may still contain other hazards, such as unspent fuel or dormant explosive packages. (Courtesy of the WSMR Museum.)

Austin L. Vick, former chief of range data collection in 1969, designed the WSMR logo. The large central star symbolically represents a significant birth in world history, both the Trinity explosion and American rocketry. The missile orbiting symbolizes America's missile and space activity, while the two groups of stars represent "4" and "5," the year of the range's founding (1945). (Courtesy of the White Sands Missile Range Public Affairs Office.)

The 49th Wing is the command organization on Holloman Air Force Base. Present at the base since 1968, the 49th flew third- and fourth-generation fighter aircraft throughout its time in New Mexico before adopting fifth-generation fighters and remotely piloted aircraft (RPAs) in the 2000s. (Courtesy of the Air Force Historical Research Agency.)

Two F-22A Raptors fly over the monument on an approach to Holloman Air Force Base. The sleek fifth-generation fighter has continued the air base's legacy of flying top-of-the-line aircraft. (Courtesy of 49th Wing Public Affairs Office.)

Pararescueman MSgt. Chris Albrand (right) escorts a teenager from an HH-60 Pavehawk on January 16, 2012. The rescue involved a 15-hour search for the missing teen, who wandered away from his family while visiting the monument. (Courtesy of 49th Wing Public Affairs Office.)

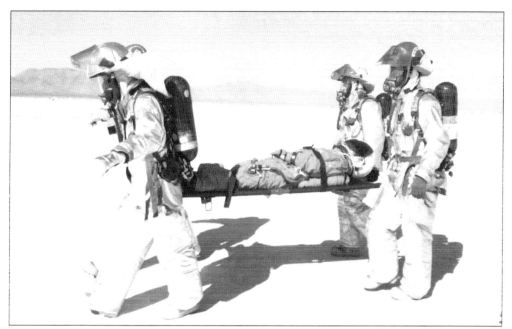

A rescue crew from Holloman AFB practices during exercises at White Sands Space Harbor (WSSH). In the event that a space shuttle would land there again, Holloman crews practice contingencies, varying from most probable to worst case. The termination of the space shuttle program in 2011 brought WSSH's usefulness to an end. (Courtesy of the 49th Wing History Office.)

The third flight of Space Shuttle *Columbia* (STS-3) lands at Northrup Strip on March 30, 1982. Pres. Ronald Reagan signed legislation on May 11, 1982, renaming Northrup Strip as White Sands Space Harbor. The 17,000-foot hard-packed gypsum was only used once in the shuttle program but remained in backup status until its closure in 2011. (Courtesy of the New Mexico Museum of Space History.)

Twenty-five F-117 Nighthawks fly over Lake Lucero as part of the 25th anniversary celebration at Holloman Air Force Base on October 27, 2006. The formation was part of the Nighthawk's 25th anniversary and 250,000 flying–hour celebration. The formation consisted of 25 planes staggered into five separate groups. (Courtesy of the 49th Wing History Office.)

Four

FLORA AND FAUNA

Like most desert environments, at first glance the dunes and surrounding flatlands of White Sands National Monument appear unpopulated, but this is a misperception. Not only is the monument teeming with life, the animals and plants of this area are uniquely adapted to live in the ever-shifting white gypsum dunes.

As with most deserts, animals that inhabit the White Sands are predominately nocturnal. During the day they rest out of the direct heat of the sun. At night the various creatures of the dunes venture out in search of food and water. One little animal, the Apache pocket mouse (*Perognathus flavescens*), is so adapted to life in the desert that, rather than searching for water, it obtains water from seeds and plants exclusively. Along with adapting to living in the desert, several species of animals have adaptive coloring; over generations, they have become predominately white to better blend in with their environment. The lesser earless lizard, *Holbrookia maculata*, displays this adaptation. At White Sands the lizard is white, while 30 miles to the north, at the lava fields, the same species is black; elsewhere throughout the Tularosa Basin, it is the traditional brown.

The plants of White Sands National Monument have also adapted to the harsh conditions of the desert. The constantly shifting sands make it difficult for plants to take root and grow quick enough to stay above the sand. The flora of White Sands must also adapt to living in an alkaline environment. Many plants have been able to adapt to the extreme conditions the monument presents. Along with the nutrient-poor soil, temperatures are extreme, reaching as high as 100 degrees or more in the summer to six degrees or below in the winter.

The *Masticophis flagellum*, common name coachwhip or Western coachwhip, is one of the more prevalent snakes in the monument. The coachwhip is nonvenomous and is typically tan or brown with a pink underbelly. This snake derives its name from its slender frame and the aggressive whipping motions it makes when captured.

Here is park ranger Sholly with a porcupine (*Erethizon dorsatum*) that had wandered into the utility area. Though wildlife is elusive within the heart of the dunes, the outlying areas are home to a variety of animals.

Most likely one of the more common lizard species that make the White Sands their home, this specimen is a meal for a *Lanius ludoviianus*, the loggerheaded shrike. The shrike is an active predator that saves future meals by impaling them on thorns or even barbed wire.

The darkling beetle, *F. Tenebrionidae*, is also known as a stink beetle. This black beetle requires no adaptive coloring to travel the dunes because, when attacked, it raises its rear and releases a noxious smelling odor. These beetles do not drink, but produce water metabolically, making them ideal desert residents.

This big-eyed creature was found in the storage room of what is now the gift shop. *Bassariscus astus*, the ring-tailed cat, is a rare creature to find in the monument. Usually buff to dark-brown, with a tail longer than its body, the ring-tailed cat prefers rocky, mountainous environments, though it is common in other parts of the Southwest.

Here is another view of a North American porcupine. In 1941, a brushfire at the foot of the neighboring San Andres Mountains sent several animals that are common in the more densely vegetated parts of the park into the outlying scrublands.

This curious fellow is a desert pocket gopher, *Geomys arenarius*. Gophers make their homes in both marginal and interior dune areas. These soft brown and gray rodents are solitary creatures. Currently, the desert pocket gopher is listed as "Near Threatened" by the International Union for the Conservation of Nature.

One of 36 species of reptiles found at White Sands, the Western diamond back, *Crotalus atrox*, is venomous. This rattlesnake can reach lengths of six feet and gives birth to live young. The distinctive diamond pattern that marks the back gives this desert-dweller its name.

Another snake, the Sonoran gopher snake (*Pituophis catenifer*), is very common in the dunes. Though not venomous, this snake gives a very convincing impression of a rattlesnake. When threatened, a gopher snake can make a rattling noise in the back of its throat while rearing up. To the untrained observer, this mimicry is convincing.

Another victim of the loggerheaded shrike, several species of lizards make White Sands National Monument their home. Of the lizards that make the dunes home, several display adaptive coloring. The bleached earless lizard, *Holbrookia maculata*, is nearly undetectable when in the gypsum dunes. The near total white coloring makes them a difficult meal for the shrike.

The strawberry hedgehog cactus, *Echinocereus stramineus*, is one of 60 plants to grow in the sands. This petite cactus is typically found in south-central New Mexico and southwest Texas. When in bloom, the flowers of these cacti are a deep pink, bordering on magenta, providing a lovely splash of color again the dusty, dry desert.

This solitary Rio Grande cottonwood, *Populus deltoides*, has made its home in an interdune area. The interdune areas along the outskirts of the dune field are some of the most densely vegetated areas of the park. The dunes in this area are slower moving, allowing plants the opportunity to take root and grow.

Another vibrant desert cactus is the claret cup hedgehog, *Echinocereus triglochidiatus*. This sister to the strawberry hedgehog cactus is pollinated predominately by hummingbirds. The vibrant deep-red flowers stay open for only three to five days in late spring, making a short but beautiful display.

Not all animals at White Sands are wild; here are Mr. Flying Bob and park ranger Alan L. Caroway patrolling the dunes. Mr. Flying Bob had an easier time maneuvering through the dunes for a patrol than any four-wheeled vehicle would. Mr. Flying Bob made it a point to make friends with visitors and enjoyed a good photograph opportunity.

The pronuba moth, *Tegeticula yuccasella*, is unique because it only pollinates yucca. Various species of yucca share a symbiotic relationship with these moths. The pronuba moth only pollinates specific species of yucca; in return, the yucca nourishes the moth's offspring.

The White Sands camel cricket, *Ammobaenites phrixocnemoides arenicolus*, displays adaptive coloring. This tiny cricket blends in perfectly with the white dunes.

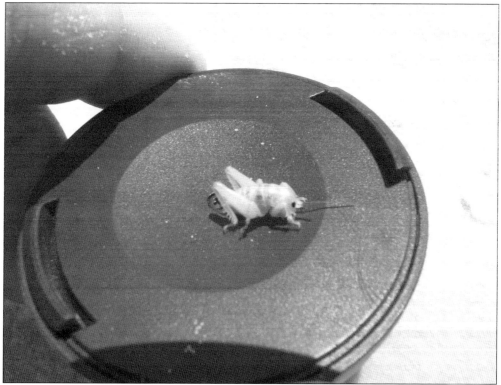

A coyote, *Canis latrans*, digs in the sand.

The purple sand verbena, *Abronia angustifolia* is common to White Sands. This nicely fragranced yet hardy plant is characterized by bright purple flowers and delicate-looking pale-green leaves. The purple sand verbena is typically found in the interdune areas of transverse and barchan dunes.

Here are Natt N. Dodge and Supt. John Faris viewing one of the majestic sand pedestals. A skunk bush sumac, *Rhus trilobata*, tops this solitary column. Sand pedestals are formed when the sand around the roots of a plant become packed. As the dunes move more, sand builds up, forcing the plant to elongate its roots to ensure that its leaves stay above the dunes.

Several varieties of hedgehog cactus make their home in the interdune areas of the monument. These cacti are frequently found along the eastern and southern boundaries of the monument, where the soil consists of gypsum and has a high alkali level. Like most desert-dwelling plants, the hedgehog cacti are drought resistant.

The state flower of New Mexico, the yucca, is abundant at White Sands. Two species of yucca make the dunes home, the soaptree yucca, *Yucca elata*, and Torrey's yucca, *Yucca torreyi*; both are capable of growing their stems more than a foot a year to keep their leaves above the dunes.

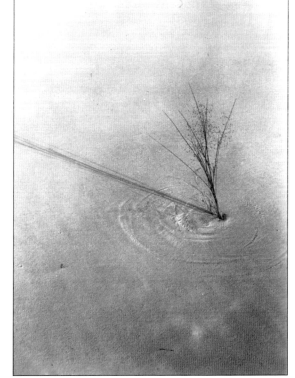

This solitary Indian ricegrass, *Achnatherum hymenoides,* is surrounded by a unique sand pattern. These are not the result of a nocturnal visitor foraging for food or of a wayward lizard; the circular patterns form when the wind lashes the stems around.

The light, feathery leaves and small pink flowers of the tamarisk, *Tamarix ramosissima*, are a beautifully deceptive mask for this invasive species. The tamarisk, also known as the salt cedar, was originally brought to the United States in the mid-1850s for use as an ornamental plant. Once released into the wild, the salt cedar quickly exploited its surroundings by guzzling down up to 200 gallons of water a day while it is actively growing, resulting in the degradation of the biome.

Goldenweed, *Xanthisma spinulosum*, is a common wild flower on the outskirts of the dunes. The small, bright-yellow flowers provide a visually pleasing accent to the otherwise dull-colored soil. During the harsh temperatures of the summer days, it is not uncommon to find bees lazily jumping from flower to flower.

This yucca is an example of *Yucca elata*. American Indians of the area used this yucca as a food source. The leaves of this plant were also used to make fiber in baskets, cloth, mats, and sandals.

Another clump of long-bladed plants have created concentric patterns in the sand. The contrast of light with dark shadows provides an interesting visual effect against the white sand.

This plant pedestal is known as "Big Pedestal." In the background are nature photographer Natt N. Dodge (left) and then-superintendent John Faris. Their presence in the picture emphasizes the grandness of the Big Pedestal. Crowning this magnificent geological structure is a Rio Grande cottonwood, *Populus deltoides*. Cottonwoods are native to the Tularosa Basin and are one of the trees that thrive at White Sands.

Mormon tea, *Ephedra torreyana*, also known as jointfir, is another plant native to the desert environment of the Southwest. Several of the compounds found in this plant are similar to those found in amphetamines. People have long used this plant to treat respiratory ailments, such as asthma and hay fever.

Here is a variety of white evening primrose. There are two varieties of white primrose at the Monument, *Oenotherea pallida runcinata* and *Oenothera pallida latifolia*. Both consist of delicate, white petals with a hint of pink. The petals are as thin as tissue paper. These flowers typically bloom in the evening

Yuccas are common at White Sands. Both varieties of yucca provided various resources to the American Indians of the area. The root of the soaptree yucca contains natural saponins and can be used to make both shampoo and soap.

This photograph of a soaptree yucca (*Yucca elata*) first appeared in the August 1935 edition of *National Geographic*. White Sands had only been a national park for a little over two years at the time. The article was an introduction to the history, science, and recreational wonders of White Sands. What had once been known only to locals and a few curious scientists was now open for the whole world to enjoy.

Taken in 1934, this photograph illustrates the stark contrast of the bleached earless lizard, *Holbrookia maculata*, with dark surroundings. The lizards forage throughout the dunes for food. On occasion, these forages lead them into the buildings that house the monument's visitor center and employees. At these times, their adaptive coloring does little to protect them from predators or cameras.

In 1973, Australian chief naturalist Bill Carter visited White Sands National Monument. The monument has always held an allure to scientists. White Sands is an ideal place for the study of evolution and what is known as the "Galápagos effect."

Most animals that make White Sands their home are nocturnal; one rarely sees them in the daytime. However, even during the day, visitors can find clues to the creatures' nighttime ramblings from their scat, half-digested meals, and tracks.

Managing to stay above the constantly shifting sands is a full-time job for plants. The small branches of this plant have managed to do just that.

Here is another picture of *Holbrookia maculata*. Often thought to be solid white, there are actually two distinct bands of color on this lizard. There are two black dorsal splotches still evident on this specimen. Many scientists the world over come to White Sands to study the various adaptive techniques that both plants and animals use to ensure their survival.

There are over 15 species of cacti that make White Sands their home. One of these is the blue barrel cactus, *Echinocactus horizonthalonius*. One of the common nicknames for this cactus in other regions is "horse maimer." The vicious, hooked needles of the blue barrel can easily puncture skin and would prove painful if stepped upon by man or beast.

Several species of raptors make the outskirts of the dune area their home. Swainson's hawk, *Buteo swainsoni*, is listed as one of the top 10 common birds at White Sands National Monument. They are sometimes referred to as a grasshopper or locust hawk, as these insects are some of its favorite meals.

White Sands National Monument is a treasure trove of science facts. The park has always taken an active role in encouraging learning, along with a healthy dose of fun. This young student on a school visit to White Sands is diligently counting the rings on a salt cedar.

The tarantula hawk wasp, *Pepsis formosa*, is a beautiful insect; its body is blue-black and accented with rust-colored, iridescent wings. The female of the species actively hunts tarantulas. Once it has acquired its prey, it will lay a single egg upon the paralyzed spider. When the egg hatches, the larva has an easy source of food.

This brightly colored brush-footed butterfly is a member of the family *Nymphalidae*. Adults feed on the nectar of flowers but also take nutrients from damp sand, of which White Sands has plenty.

Taken in 1940, this photograph is of Natt N. Dodge (back) and Supt. Johnwill Faris (front). Natt N. Dodge was a prolific photographer of the Southwest. He published several works on various Southwest wildlife and flora. During his visits to the Southwest, he captured amazing photographs that are seen in the archives of numerous parks.

Five

SKY AND SANDSCAPES

The ever-shifting dunes of White Sands National Monument have long inspired artists and dreamers. The amazing play of colors encourages visitors to stop and contemplate the wonders of nature. Many artists have traveled around the world to arrive at the foot of the dunes in an attempt to capture the beautiful starkness of crisp white dunes against a vivid blue sky on a cloudless day. During a moonless night, White Sands provides a clean, sparkling view of the stars, like diamonds against black velvet. The monument is a great place to view celestial activities such as lunar and solar eclipses, meteor showers, and the ever-wonderful full moon. During these events, White Sands will remain open late into the night to allow visitors a chance to enjoy the sight of the flawless skies against the white dunes. One popular event is Full Moon Night, when the monument remains open for visitors and photographers well into the night. It is not uncommon to wander through the dunes and come across an intrepid photographer working to capture a beautiful cloud scene with the dunes in the foreground or working during a full moon to convey the beauty of the dunes turned silver through the lens of a camera.

White Sands National Monument is comprised of several types of dunes: barchan, parabolic, transverse, and dome. The fastest moving are the dome dunes, which can move up to 30 feet per year. Each dune field across the world varies in the life it supports and the beauty it displays. White Sands National Monument is the only place on earth where one can experience the stark contrast of white dunes against a vivid blue sky, accented by a yucca in full bloom. The monument's scenery is so stunning and unique that every year various agencies travel to the monument to film commercials, perform photo shoots, and even film movies.

Cottonwoods are native to the Tularosa Basin. Though they prefer soil and valleys with fresh water, cottonwoods have managed to survive at White Sands National Monument through perseverance and adaptation to the surrounding dune environment.

The beauty of the dunes encourages introspection. Here, Private First Class Colburn takes a moment on the dunes to reflect.

A cottonwood in the foreground offers a break in the view of the San Andres Mountains.

At the crest of this dune, the tips of a few plants are silhouetted against the sky. The visible tracks in the dunes display a recent wind pattern.

This dead cottonwood offers an appealing foreground subject against the sky. Though no longer decorated with green leaves, the gnarled, far-reaching branches provide shade and homes for wandering wildlife. Such views are not uncommon; the struggle to acquire fresh water and stay rooted in the shifting sands can be too much for the plants that make this their home.

At first glance, this bone-white piece of wood, similar to driftwood, could make one believe that the ocean might be waiting on the other side of the dunes. Instead, there is a vast, white expanse of more dunes, with no surface water in sight.

Once more, the wind has etched the dunes with a unique pattern. The ripple-like waves are created when the wind blows the top layer of loose gypsum and the minute crystals pile up against one another, anchoring together to form tiny ripples in the sand.

These unique structures are called crystal domes, or crystal pedestals. They are unique to the monument and to Mars. They have been created at Alkali Flats and are believed to have been caused by upwelling of mineral water.

In 1974, a record amount of snow was recorded at White Sands National Monument—eight inches in a day. Here is water that had been flowing through the roof drainage system. As snow melted on the roof, runoff would occur, only to freeze again that night as temperatures dropped.

Sunset and sunrise are two of the most beautiful times of day to enjoy White Sands. Never the same twice, the colors of the sky can vary from the palest shades of blue and pink to intense crimson and indigo.

Miniature lagoons form in the low parts of the dune area during heavy rainfall. The nature of the high water table, only a foot or two below the dunes, allows water to pool. It can be several days or even months before the water completely evaporates or is absorbed into the ground.

An aerial view of the picnic area at White Sands National Monument shows the great expanse of dunes in the distance. Every year, thousands upon thousands of people visit to play and picnic in the dunes.

Looking like a desert expanse in another country, the dunes offer a different view from the normal brown, dusty desert floor.

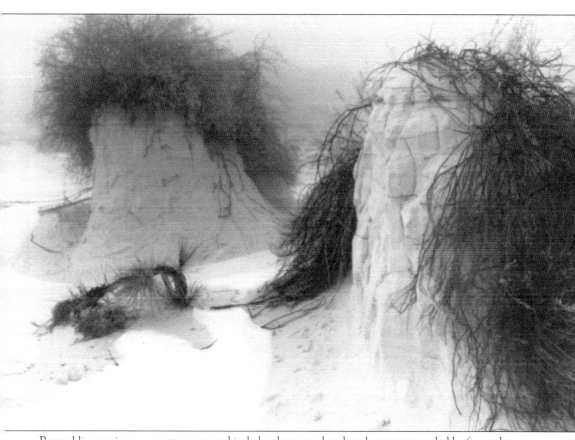

Resembling eerie sea monsters covered in kelp, these sand pedestals are surrounded by fog and snow. On such an occasion, variations of white are visible when comparing the sand to the snow.

Taken in the Dune Life Nature Trail area, this photograph shows a full moon starting to peak out over the dunes. During full-moon nights, the public is invited to glimpse a different view of the sands. The normal, glaring-white dunes take on an almost silver, crystalline appearance.

The heart of the dunes offers the best in the way of sledding. The dunes in this area are vegetation-free, rolling, and steep, offering the perfect incline for sledding with one of the plastic discs sold from the gift shop, or even a piece of waxed cardboard.

The dunes in this photograph appear as if they are waiting for the tide to roll in.

With sumac adorning the top of the sand pedestals and a lone yucca in the foreground, this photograph resembles the entrance to a maze. It is fairly easy to become disoriented in the dune field. Visitors are encouraged to stay within sight of their vehicles or on a marked park trail.

This photograph was taken on Easter weekend in 1936. It is not retouched, but shows plainly the true beauty of the landscape of the monument.

This structure has been formed by years of erosion by wind and water. Though not common in the interdune areas, structures like this one can be found in flat outer areas, particularly near the source of the White Sands, Lake Lucero.

Here is a close-up of mirabilite crystal formation at the small playa along Dunes Drive. Prior to the establishment of the monument, a small gypsum brick mill existed on the outskirts of the dune field, manufacturing bricks for homes in the Tularosa Basin.

This is another view of the formation of mirabilite crystals. Mirabilite is unstable in dry air, and readily decomposes into white powder called thenardite.

When the seasonal rains arrive, small ponds can be found throughout the monument. On occasion, enough rain can build up that the roads into the monument can become unsafe. At that time, the park closes part or all of the road until the water evaporates or drains to a more manageable level.

In the background loom the sharp San Andres Mountains. Over these mountains lies the city of Las Cruces, and at the base is White Sands Missile Range. A portion of the dunes lies within the WSMR jurisdiction and is not accessible to the public.

White Sands National Monument is not entirely made up of rolling dunes of white gypsum. Within the boundaries of the monument are shrub lands, fossilized dune areas, playas, and other desert biomes. These areas include a diversity of plant and animal life and some contain interesting, eye catching patterns such as this 20,000-year-old mammoth trackway on Alkali Flats.

In one of the more densely-vegetated areas of the monument, one can see various shrubs and grasses growing at the base of the dunes. The more vegetation, the more variety of wildlife there will be. Mammals, birds, and other small critters frequent areas like this.

Nature plays a vital role in the variation seen within the dunes. The amount of wind and moisture play a role in how the sand will form. The unique dune formation seen here is the result of the top layers of sand being saturated with moisture, compacted, and then blown away.

The monsoon season lasts through the late summer months, bringing much needed rain to the desert. In the background are thunderclouds rolling over the Sacramento Mountains.

With the San Andres Mountains in the background, the *playa*, or dry lakebed, of Lake Lucero is visible. Lake Lucero is the source of White Sands.

These "trails" are commonly referred to as dune footprints. They are left behind as a dune moves forward. Wind patterns in the dunes vary depending on the weather. Rain, wind, and sun all contribute to the unique varieties of dune patterns.

With no mountain ranges visible
in the background, this view could
be from anywhere. Individuals
who find themselves lost in the
dunes are encouraged to make
it to the top of a dune and stay
put, rather than risk becoming
disoriented and even more lost.

From the peak of this dune, it is
easy to see how a person could
get lost in thought and wander
away from civilization. The dunes
attract artists throughout the year
searching for a chance to turn
inward and express themselves.

Low clouds enhance the view of this temporary lake. The vegetation in this bowl will take what it needs to survive. The remaining water will slowly evaporate, leaving behind a crust of minerals that will eventually break down and be swept out into the dunes.

Every year, people from around the world wake up at the crack of dawn to witness the rise of hot air balloons from White Sands National Monument. The gates open before sunrise for eager photographers and viewers to find the perfect spot to catch the many vibrant hues of the balloons against the dunes.

At left, a young girl runs playfully through the monument; below, a name is scrawled into white sand. Like the message itself, the visitor's presence within the monument is only temporary; however, it is hoped that the experience at White Sands National Monument, whether scientific or spiritual, penetrates every visitor, leaving an indelible mark on their souls. (Left, courtesy of Page family, New Mexico chapter; below, courtesy of Erin E. Gaberlavage.)

The sun sets in the western skies, blanketing the reflective gypsum sands of White Sands National Monument. (Courtesy of Erin E. Gaberlavage.)

BIBLIOGRAPHY

Atkinson, Richard. *White Sands: Wind, Sand and Time*. Globe, AZ: Southwest Parks and Monuments Association, 1977.

Hudnall, Ken and Sharon. *Spirits of the Border: The History and the Mystery of New Mexico*. El Paso, TX: Omega Press, 2005.

Page II, Joseph T. *Holloman Air Force Base*. Charleston, SC: Arcadia Publishing, 2012.

———. *New Mexico Space Trail*. Charlston, SC: Arcadia Publishing, 2013.

Schneider-Hector, Dietmar. *White Sands: The History of a National Monument*. Albuquerque, NM: University of New Mexico Press, 1993.

Welsh, Michael. *Dunes and Dreams: A History of White Sands National Monument*. Santa Fe, NM: Intermountain Cultural Resource Center Professional Paper No. 55. National Park Service, 1995.

About the White Sands National Monument

White Sands National Monument is one of the over 400 parks in the National Park System. Located in the heart of the Tularosa Basin, along New Mexico's Highway 70, many activities take place at WSNM over the course of the year, including the following:

Sunset Strolls: This is a stroll through the dunes to look at the geology, plants, and animals of the dune field. The walk is timed to end at sunset in order to provide good photographic opportunities.

Sunrise Photography: This early-morning program is focused on amateur or novice photographers taking great pictures in the early-morning light.

Skins and Skulls: Rangers give a brief talk about the 44 different species of mammals that live at the monument and have pelts, skulls, and other props to provide an up-close look and feel of the monument's elusive wildlife.

Patio Talks: A ranger presents a short 20 minute talk on the visitor center patio on a variety of topics about the Monument.

Balloon Invitational: Enjoy the sight of colorful hot-air balloons launching from the snow-white gypsum dunes during the annual White Sands Balloon Invitational. The annual September event begins right at sunrise, in the heart of the dunes, and lasts until the balloons come down.

Holiday Open House: For one night only out of the year, 1,000 luminaries illuminate the historic adobe visitor center with live music, complimentary light hors d'oeuvres, hot cider, and hot chocolate, along with holiday sales in the bookstore and gift shop.

Full-Moon Hikes: From May through October, rangers lead a unique night hike through the monument under the glow of a full moon. Reservations are required and can only be made via website two weeks in advance of the scheduled hike.

Lake Lucero Tours: Learn about the formation of the sands and the special plants and animals that live in and around the dunes. These tours are only offered once a month from November through April.

Some events have additional fees beyond normal park entrance fees. Schedules are subject to change, call to confirm dates and times. Activities may be cancelled due to weather or missile range activities. For information call (575) 479-6124 or visit www.nps.gov/whsa.

White Sands National Monument
P.O. Box 1086
Holloman AFB, NM, 88330-1086
(575) 479-6124
www.nps.gov/whsa

Discover Thousands of Local History Book
Featuring Millions of Vintage Images

Arcadia Publishing, the leading local history publisher in the United States, is committed to making history accessible and meaningful through publishing books that celebrate and preserve the heritage of America's people and places.

Find more books like this at
www.arcadiapublishing.com

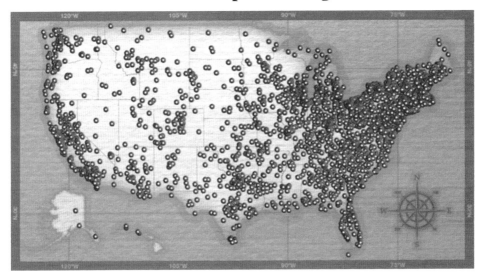

Search for your hometown history, your old stomping grounds, and even your favorite sports team.

Consistent with our mission to preserve history on a local level, this book was printed in South Carolina on American-made paper and manufactured entirely in the United States. Products carrying the accredited Forest Stewardship Council (FSC) label are printed on 100 percent FSC-certified paper.

MADE IN THE USA